Felt Accessories

NO LONGER PROPERTY OF
KING COUNTY LIBRARY SYSTEM

SEP   2007

make it in
Minutes

Felt Accessories

TAYLOR HAGERTY

LARK BOOKS

A Division of Sterling Publishing Co., Inc.
New York / London

Book Editor
Rebecca Ittner

Copy Editors
Lisa Anderson
Catherine Risling

Photographer
Zachary Williams
Williams Visual
Ogden, UT

Stylist
Brittany Aardema

Book Designer
Kehoe + Kehoe Design
Associates, Inc.
Burlington, VT

Other Books
in this Series:

Make It in Minutes:
Greeting Cards

Make It in Minutes:
Mini-Books

Make It in Minutes:
Mini-Boxes

Make It in Minutes:
Beaded Jewelry

Make It in Minutes:
Party Favors
& Hostess Gifts

A Red Lips 4 Courage Communications, Inc. book
www.redlips4courage.com

Eileen Cannon Paulin
President

Catherine Risling
Director of Editorial

Library of Congress Cataloging-in-Publication Data
Hagerty, Taylor.
    Make It in minutes. Felt accessories / Taylor Hagerty.
    1st ed. p. cm. – (Make It in minutes)
    Includes index.
ISBN-13: 978-1-60059-127-3 (hc-plc concealed spiral : alk. paper)
ISBN-10: 1-60059-127-2 (hc-plc concealed spiral : alk. paper)
1. Felt work. I. Title.
TT849.5.H35 2007
746'.0463--dc22
                                                    2007008661

10 9 8 7 6 5 4 3 2 1
First Edition

Published by Lark Books, A Division of
Sterling Publishing Co., Inc.
387 Park Avenue South, New York, NY 10016

Text © 2007, Taylor Hagerty
Photography © 2007, Red Lips 4 Courage Communications, Inc.
Illustrations © 2007, Red Lips 4 Courage Communications, Inc.

Distributed in Canada by Sterling Publishing,
c/o Canadian Manda Group, 165 Dufferin Street
Toronto, Ontario, Canada M6K 3H6

Distributed in the United Kingdom by GMC Distribution Services,
Castle Place, 166 High Street, Lewes, East Sussex, England BN7 1XU

Distributed in Australia by Capricorn Link (Australia) Pty Ltd.,
P.O. Box 704, Windsor, NSW 2756 Australia

The written instructions, photographs, designs, patterns, and projects in this volume are intended for the personal use of the reader and may be reproduced for that purpose only. Any other use, especially commercial use, is forbidden under law without written permission of the copyright holder.

Every effort has been made to ensure that all the information in this book is accurate. However, due to differing conditions, tools, and individual skills, the publisher cannot be responsible for any injuries, losses, and other damages that may result from the use of the information in this book.

If you have questions or comments about this book, please contact:
Lark Books
67 Broadway
Asheville, NC 28801
(828) 253-0467

Manufactured in China
All rights reserved

ISBN 13: 978-1-60059-127-3
ISBN 10: 1-60059-127-2

For information about custom editions, special sales, premium and corporate purchases, please contact Sterling Special Sales Department at (800) 805-5489 or specialsales@sterlingpub.com.

"Create your own visual style...let it be for yourself and yet identifiable for others."
—Orson Welles

Contents

Introduction

Look around you and notice the small accessories that are used over and over, like your key chain, mouse pad, or wallet. Accessories can dress up an outfit, a desk, or a room. In our hurry-up world, surrounding yourself with these personal touches makes every day more enjoyable.

Creating unique and beautiful felted wool accessories to suit any style is fun and easy. In this book you will find easy-to-create projects to beautify every facet of your life, from your home office to the kitchen table. You also will find some that are perfect for gift-giving.

After familiarizing yourself with some basic supplies, stitches, and techniques, you will be creating felted wool accessories and gifts with a personal flair that are sure to turn everyday details into extraordinary ones.

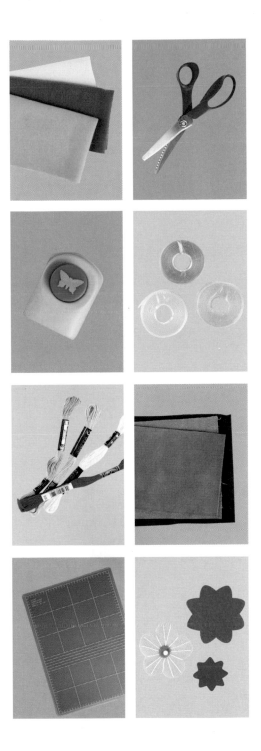

CHAPTER 1

Nearly everything you need to create the projects in this book can be found at your local craft or fabric store. Some felt, particularly felted wool and 100 percent wool felt, can be found at quilt shops. The Internet is also a wonderful source for supplies.

Before embarking on the projects in this book, you will want to become familiar with the basic techniques, supplies, and tools in this chapter. You may also want to familiarize yourself with the various types of felt. Craft felt is easy to find and will work with every project, but if you want to work with the softest felt and the most luscious colors, consider using felted wool or 100 percent wool felt. Once familiar with the supplies and techniques, you will be ready to create beautiful, handmade felted wool accessories.

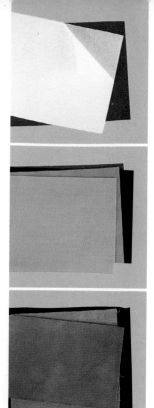

Felt

Adhesive-backed craft felt
Readily available at craft stores, adhesive-backed craft felt comes in a variety of colors. It is used to add shape, strength, and stiffness to projects.

Craft felt
Also readily available at craft stores, craft felt comes in a variety of colors, textures, and weights. It is an inexpensive alternative to wool felt and felted wool.

Felted wool
Felted wool is woven woolen yardage that has been subjected to the fulling process. Made of 100 percent wool, felted wool is the top-of-the-line felt and is perfect for small projects.

Wool felt
Made of 100 percent wool, wool felt is readily available in fabric stores and online. It is stiffer and heavier than felted wool and is available in a wide range of colors.

Wool felt blends
Wool felt blends are made of unwoven wool and other fibers that are bonded together through the use of moisture, heat, soap, and friction or pressure. Most wool felt blends for crafting are 20 percent wool and 80 percent rayon. Manufacturers may call these products wool felt.

time-saving tip

Fulling on a Budget
Fulling refers to the simple machine washing and drying process by which wool fabric becomes felted wool. Finding wool to felt is as easy as looking in your closet or the nearest thrift store. Choose garments made of 100 percent wool and take each piece apart prior to washing, making sure to remove buttons, zippers, snaps, etc.

Materials

Adhesive-backed magnets
Adhesive-backed magnets are available in a variety of shapes including dots, squares, and strips. They can be adhered to the back of small projects to easily create decorative magnets.

Bar pins
Bar pins can be sewn or glued to the back of small felted items to ready them for wearing, like the lapel pin project.

Beading thread
This thin, strong thread is made especially for beading. Use with beading needles to secure beads to project surfaces. Available in a variety of colors and thicknesses.

Beads
Beads add a decorative flair and elegance to any project. They are adhered in a variety of ways including gluing, pinning, and sewing. They also can be strung on embroidery floss or ribbon.

Brads
Brads are available in all colors, shapes, and sizes. They can be used to secure pieces of felt together or as decorations. To adhere, simply push the closed prongs through a pre-punched hole, spread open the prongs, and flatten to the back to secure.

Buttons
Buttons add the perfect finishing touch to handmade projects. They can also be used to cover stitching, fastener backs, and other mechanics. Sew or glue buttons on material to adhere.

time-saving tip

Get Ready
Gather all necessary tools and materials before starting a project. Having everything on hand will make for a more enjoyable crafting experience.

13

Cardstock
Cardstock provides shape and stiffness to projects when placed between layers of felt. It is easy to sew through.

Charms

Charms are available in a variety of themes. Made from a range of materials including metal and plastic, charms can be glued or sewn onto projects or can be dangled from ribbons or embroidery floss.

Embroidery floss

Embroidery floss is made up of six strands, which can be divided to give whatever thickness is required. Readily available at craft and fabric stores, embroidery floss is sold in skeins and is available in a wide variety of colors, including variegated.

Eyelets

Eyelets are made of metal and can be used as decoration or as openings through which to tie ribbons or floss for closure. Available in a wide variety of colors, shapes, and sizes, eyelets are set in place with eyelet setting tools.

Fusible web
Fusible web is a man-made fiber that melts when heated. It is used to fuse pieces of felt together. Available at fabric and craft stores, fusible web comes in rolls of various widths, by the yard, and in pre-packaged pieces.

Heavyweight interfacing
Heavyweight interfacing adds sturdiness and durability to projects. It can also be cut into shapes and used for embellishment. It can be sewn onto projects or adhered using fusible web.

Using Scrap Materials time-saving tip
To save time and money, use leftover materials such as felt, ribbon, and beads from previous crafting projects.

O-rings

Readily available at craft and office supply stores, o-rings provide an attachment point for keys, ribbons, charms, and more. O-rings are available in a wide variety of colors and sizes.

Post-style snaps

Post-style snaps have a shaft that pokes through a pre-punched hole. They must be set using a snap attacher tool.

Potpourri

Potpourri has long been a home décor favorite. Potpourri can also be used as a scented filler, like in the sachet project.

Prong snaps

Prong snaps are snap fasteners with teeth that penetrate through fabric. They are available in a variety of styles, including open rings, gems, and decorative finishes. Prong snaps add a decorative element to projects as well as work as a closure.

Ready-made felt appliqués

Ready-made felt appliqués come in a variety of colors, shapes, and sizes. Adhesive-backed appliqués are also available.

Rhinestones

Rhinestones add an elegant sparkle to projects. Available in a variety of colors, shapes, and sizes, rhinestones are adhered to projects with craft glue. Some rhinestones come with adhesive backing.

time-saving tip

Hiding Imperfections

Rhinestones and sequins not only add sparkle and dimension to projects, they can also provide the perfect cover up for misplaced stitches or other imperfections.

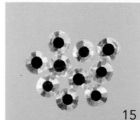

Ribbon

Ribbon can be used to stitch layers of felt together, or for embellishment. By sewing a length of ribbon to the ends or the back of a project, ribbons can also be used to tie projects closed, as seen on the knitting needle and notepad holder projects.

Rice

A staple in every home, rice can be used a variety of ways, including as a filler for the felt paperweight project.

Sequins

Sequins are available in a variety of colors, shapes, and sizes. Use them to add a bit of sparkle to a project or under beads to help hold them in place. They can be sewn or glued to projects.

Sew-on post-style snaps

Sew-on post-style snaps have a shaft that pokes through a pre-punched hole in a piece of fabric. They are sewn onto fabric with embroidery floss or thread.

Temporary spray adhesive

Temporary spray adhesive is used to hold pieces of a project in place before final stitching.

Twine

Widely available in craft stores, twine is used to tie projects closed.

Additional Supplies

These everyday items will help you craft felted wool accessories:

- Computer and printer
- Copier
- Copier paper
- Paper clips
- Toothpicks

Tools and Supplies

Beading needles

Chenille needles

Craft knife

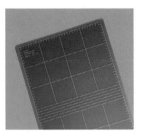

Craft mat

Craft punch

Craft scissors

Decorative-edge scissors

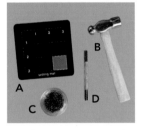

Eyelet setting tools
A Setting mat   C Eyelets
B Craft hammer   D Eyelet setter

Fabric glue

Fabric marking pencil

Funnel

Hole punch

Hot-glue gun

Hot-glue sticks

Iron

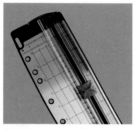

Paper trimmer

Pinking shears

Pressing cloth

Seam sealer

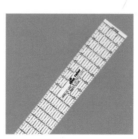

See-through ruler

Self-adhesive hook-and-loop dots

Snap attacher tool

Straight pins

White craft glue

Stitches

■ *Blanket stitch:* Bring needle to front on lower line; insert needle at top, a bit to the right (A). Bring needle out directly below, making sure to keep thread under needle tip (B). Pull thread through felt, over top of working thread. Pull thread to form a firm loop at lower line (C). Continue as above, making sure to space stitches evenly and at same height.

■ *Long and short blanket stitch:* Work the same way as with blanket stitch, but alternate long and short upright stitches.

■ *Buttonhole stitch:* Working on two parallel lines, bring needle out at bottom left. Insert needle directly above on top line then bring it out on bottom line a bit to the right, keeping thread under needle tip.

■ *Closed buttonhole stitch:* Working on two parallel lines, start at bottom left. Insert needle to right on top line and bring out on bottom line, slanting to left, and making sure working thread is under needle tip (A). Pull thread through, insert needle at top of previous stitch, and then make another stitch slanting to right, creating a triangle shape (B). Pull needle through gently, completing first closed buttonhole stitch, and making sure thread is under needle tip (C). Repeat, spacing stitches evenly.

Blanket stitch

Long and short blanket stitch

Buttonhole stitch

Closed buttonhole stitch

19

Chain stitch

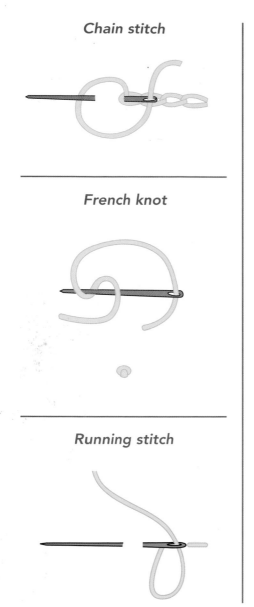

French knot

Running stitch

■ *Chain stitch:* Work down along a single stitching line. Bring thread through to front at top of stitching line. Form thread into loop, hold loop in place with thumb, and then re-insert needle in same hole. Hold thread loop with thumb and bring needle tip to front, one stitch length from starting point. With loop under needle, pull needle through to make first chain. Form loop of thread, insert needle next to emerging thread, and then bring needle tip out one stitch length away. Pull needle through overworking thread, making second chain. Continue on.

■ *French knot:* Work two tiny stitches at back of fabric. Bring thread through to front of fabric. Hold thread taut and wrap it around needle. Pull thread to gently tighten twists around needle. While holding thread taut, insert needle into felt, close to point where it emerged. Pull needle and thread to back of fabric, leaving loose knot at front. Work two tiny stitches at back to tie off.

■ *Running stitch:* Bring needle to front at starting point. Pass needle in and out of fabric along stitching line, working several stitches at a time.

Note: A primitive running stitch is a running stitch where stitches are spaced further apart and are not even.

time-saving tip

Tension Matters

To ensure that projects lay flat, make sure not to pull your thread too tight. Keeping the tension of the thread constant as you move from stitch to stitch will result in a neat, smooth surface.

Techniques

Setting an eyelet

To set eyelets in felt, make a small hole in the felt where the eyelet is to be set using a hole punch. Insert the eyelet through the hole and position the project face down on a craft mat. Using a setting tool and hammer, flatten the eyelet's back side to secure it in place. *Note:* Some eyelet setting systems vary; simply follow the manufacturer's instructions.

Setting a prong fastener

There are four pieces that make up a prong fastener, from top to bottom: the top prong ring, the socket, the stud, and the open prong ring. Push the prongs of the top prong ring through the felt, then snap the socket onto the prongs. Push the prongs of the open prong ring up through the bottom piece of fabric and snap the stud onto the prongs.

Setting snap fastener

Place project on craft mat. Set shaft piece in cup, set fabric over shaft, and place matching piece on top. Place anvil over piece and strike with hammer.

Using fusible web

Cut felt and fusible web to size. Layer fusible web between layers of felt. Lay pressing cloth onto felt. Press felt, melting web and fusing layers together.

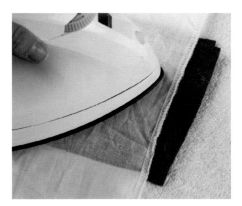

Felting (fulling) wool

Fulling wool shrinks the wool from 15–25 percent. Begin with 100 percent wool fabric. (Sort colors and wash them separately.)

Instructions

1. Wash wool in hot water on the regular cycle, using a small amount of detergent. *Important:* Do not use detergent with bleach additives. Bleach disintegrates wool.

2. Run fabric through an additional rinse cycle.

3. Dry fabric in dryer on medium setting. Place a terrycloth towel and a dryer sheet in with the wool. The towel will felt the wool a little more and the dryer sheet will increase softness.

CHAPTER 2

With many of your waking hours spent working, having an inviting work environment is essential. Maybe you've been in the same office for awhile and are just bored with the generic store-bought décor and organizers that fill your space. Perhaps you just painted the walls and moved in. Transform your office in minutes with easy-to-create projects that lend individual style to every corner. Imagine sitting down at your desk and seeing a beautiful mouse pad or opening a binder to find a handsome pencil case. Creating a space filled with accessories that infuse a calming and welcoming feel to this all-important room is simple. From a cozy coffee cup holder to an elegant business card case, the ideas found in this chapter will make your work day enjoyable.

Business Card Holder

Materials

- Adhesive-backed craft felt: white
- Charms (3)
- Chenille needle: size 20
- Craft felt: blue
- Craft glue
- Craft mat
- Craft scissors
- Embroidery floss: metallic gold
- Fabric marker pencil
- Hole punch
- Prong snap
- Ruler
- Trim: gold

Instructions

Note: All stitching is done with six strands of embroidery floss.

1. Cut two 4½" x 7" pieces of blue felt, and two of same size from white felt.

2. Peel backing off one piece of white felt, line up edges with one piece of blue felt, and finger press to secure pieces together. Repeat with remaining felt pieces.

3. Place one piece, blue side down, on craft mat. Mark ten evenly spaced holes ⅜" in from edge along both 4¼" sides. Punch hole at each marked spot. Fold piece in half again, blue side out, and slip remaining piece into fold. Line up edges and mark hole placement on first piece. Punch holes in first piece, slide it into folded piece, and then stitch pieces together through holes.

4. Embellish flap of case with charms adhered to outside. Sew snap on underside of flap and front of case.

5. Turn over card holder. Glue trim onto back pocket, wrapping edges of ribbon behind side edges of pocket.

Mouse Pad

Materials

- Adhesive-backed craft felt: light blue
- Adhesive-backed felt embellishments: large flower, medium flower, small flower
- Beads: glass (2)
- Chenille needle: size 20
- Craft mat
- Craft scissors
- Embroidery floss: green
- Fabric marker pencil
- Felted wool: green
- Hole punch
- Paper trimmer
- Ribbon
- Ruler
- Scissors: craft, pinking shears

Instructions

1. Using paper trimmer, cut one 8" square from blue felt. Using pinking shears, cut one 8" square from green felt.

2. Remove backing from large flower embellishment and stitch to corner of green felt, ½" in from edge. Remove backing from remaining two flower embellishments and wrap embroidery floss around medium flower. Layer small flower on medium flower, then place medium flower on large flower. Finger press to secure.

3. Glue beads on top of flower embellishment.

4. Remove backing from light blue felt, line up edge with green felt, and finger press together to secure.

5. Mark seven evenly spaced holes along each side, ¼" in from edge. Punch hole at each marked spot.

6. Thread ribbon through holes all along perimeter. Tie knot at last hole; trim ribbon ends.

time-saving tip

Keep it Simple

To save time, cut two same-size pieces of adhesive-backed craft felt. Remove the backing and finger press the pieces together to secure.

Pen Holder

Materials

- Adhesive-backed craft felt: white
- Chenille needle: size 20
- Craft felt: blue, green
- Craft mat
- Craft scissors
- Embroidery floss: green
- Fabric marker pencil
- Hole punch
- Ribbon
- Ruler
- Snap attacher tool
- Snap fastener
- Straight pins

Instructions

Note: All stitching is done with six strands of embroidery floss.

1. Cut one 3½" x 9¼" rectangle from blue felt.

2. Cut one 3½" x 7" rectangle from green felt and one 3½" x 6¾" rectangle from white felt.

3. Remove backing from white felt. Line up bottom edge with bottom edge of blue felt and finger press to secure.

4. Line up bottom edge of green felt with bottom edge of blue felt and pin pieces to hold in place.

5. Using blanket stitch, stitch around perimeter of pen case. Tie off.

6. Embellish flap of case with ribbon bow sewn to outside and snap fastener to underside of flap and front of case.

time-saving tip

Use an Alternative Closure

Self-adhesive hook-and-loop dots would also work well as a closure for the pen holder. Just secure the dots with a couple of stitches.

Pencil Case

Materials

- Binder: three-ring
- Buttons (3)
- Chenille needle: size 20
- Craft felt: 8½" x 10" black heavyweight
- Embroidery floss: black
- Eyelet setting tools
- Eyelets: medium (2); small star-shaped
- Fabric marker pencil
- Hole punch
- Iron
- Pinking shears
- Pressing cloth
- Ribbon (8")
- Ruler
- Self-adhesive hook-and-loop dots (3)

Instructions

Note: All stitching is done with six strands of embroidery floss.

1. Fold 8½" bottom edge of black felt up, stopping 1" from top edge. Press seam with iron, using pressing cloth.

2. Trim top and bottom edges with pinking shears. Using blanket stitch, stitch side edges closed.

3. Punch three evenly spaced holes on top flap, ½" from top edge. Set eyelet in each hole. Weave ribbon through holes; tie off ribbons on backside of eyelets.

4. Stitch buttons on flap, one in center and one at each end of flap.

5. Open flap. Mark placement for self-adhesive hook-and-loop dots. Place dots on marks and secure with a couple of stitches around edges of each dot. Close flap.

6. Place pencil case next to rings in binder and mark placement for eyelets.

7. Punch holes where marked. Set eyelet in each hole.

time-saving tip

Variety of Uses

The pencil case is the perfect place to store small items, such as notepads or address books, that you need to keep on hand.

Sea Star Paperweight

Materials

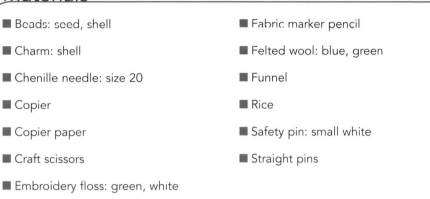

- Beads: seed, shell
- Charm: shell
- Chenille needle: size 20
- Copier
- Copier paper
- Craft scissors
- Embroidery floss: green, white
- Fabric marker pencil
- Felted wool: blue, green
- Funnel
- Rice
- Safety pin: small white
- Straight pins

Instructions

Note: All stitching is done with six strands of embroidery floss.

1. Photocopy Large Sea Star Template (page 116) twice; cut out template and pin to blue felt. Cut out shapes. Remove pins and template.

2. Photocopy Small Sea Star Template (page 116); cut out template and pin to green felt. Cut out shape. Remove pins and template.

3. Pin small star to one large star and attach using a running stitch.

4. String two shell beads, one shell charm, and then two more shell beads onto safety pin. Stitch safety pin to small star with white embroidery floss, as shown.

5. Attach one shell bead and one seed bead to each corner of small star using white embroidery floss, as shown.

6. Pin two large stars together and stitch around outer edges, leaving a small opening. Insert funnel into opening and pour rice into star. Stitch opening closed. Remove pins.

time-saving tip
Fill It Up
Buckwheat also may be used to fill the paperweight. Add some dried lavender to the filler for a pleasing scent.

Note Card Holder

Materials

- Beads: clear (2)
- Brads: square black (2)
- Chenille needle: size 20
- Copier
- Copier paper
- Craft scissors
- Embroidery floss: black
- Fabric marker pencil
- Ruler
- Straight pins
- Wool felt: blue, gold, green, red

Instructions

Note: All stitching is done with six strands of embroidery floss.

1. Photocopy Note Card Flower Template (page 117); cut out template and pin to green felt. Cut out shape. Remove pins and template.

2. Photocopy Small Circle Template (page 117) twice; cut out templates and pin to red felt. Cut out shapes. Remove pins and templates.

3. Photocopy Large Leaf and Small Leaf templates (page 117); cut out templates and pin to green felt. Cut out shapes. Remove pins and templates.

4. Cut one 6¼" x 5¼" rectangle and one 6¼" x 3½" rectangle from blue felt. Cut corners off smaller rectangle, creating front flap. Cut one 6¼" x 4" rectangle from green felt.

5. Pin flower and leaf shapes to front flap. Stitch in place with running stitch. Attach one red circle to center of flower with brad.

6. Pin green rectangle to bottom of blue rectangle and blanket stitch around outer edges. Blanket stitch around flap and then across top, connecting flap to note card holder. Attach red circle to green rectangle with brad. String one bead onto each end of 12" length of black embroidery floss; knot ends. Wrap length of embroidery floss around red circles and tie into bow.

Coffee Cup Holder

Materials

- Chenille needle: size 20
- Copier
- Copier paper
- Craft felt: gold, tan
- Craft scissors
- Elastic: $\frac{1}{4}$" x 1" (3)

- Embroidery floss: black, brown, tan
- Fabric glue
- Straight pins
- Tulle: ivory
- Wool felt: brown, dark red

Instructions

Note: All stitching is done with six strands of embroidery floss.

1. Photocopy Coffee Cup Holder Template (page 117) twice; cut out templates and pin one to brown felt and one to dark red felt. Cut out shapes. Remove pins and templates.

2. Photocopy Beehive Template (page 118); cut out template and pin to tan felt. Cut out shape. Remove pins and template.

3. Photocopy Bee Template (page 118) three times; cut out templates and pin to gold felt. Cut out shapes. Remove pins and templates.

4. Photocopy Wing Template (page 118) six times; cut out templates and pin to ivory tulle. Cut out shapes. Remove pins and templates.

5. Position bees and beehive on brown felt and secure each with a dot of glue. Using tan embroidery floss, sew on beehive. Using black embroidery floss, sew on bees. Position wings and sew onto bees with black embroidery floss.

6. Layer coffee cup holders; using blanket stitch, stitch long sides together with brown embroidery floss. Attach ends of elastic pieces to each short side; using blanket stitch, stitch short sides closed.

time-saving tip
Color Matters
Use dark-colored felt for the coffee cup holder to hide any coffee stains.

Heart Magnet

Materials

- Adhesive-backed magnet: small round
- Beads: silver (6)
- Charm: open heart
- Chenille needle: size 20
- Copier
- Copier paper
- Craft scissors
- Embroidery floss: red
- Ribbon: ⅜"-wide silk
- Straight pins
- Wool felt: ecru, red

Instructions

Note: All stitching is done with six strands of embroidery floss.

1. Photocopy Large Heart Template (page 118) twice; cut out templates and pin to ecru felt. Cut out shapes. Remove pins and templates.

2. Photocopy Medium Heart Template (page 118); cut out template and pin to red felt. Cut out shape. Remove pins and template.

3. Pin red heart to one ecru heart and blanket stitch around outer edge of red heart.

4. Pin large hearts together and blanket stitch around outer edges to join.

5. Tie ribbon in bow and stitch in place with charm. Lace beads up ribbon and tie knot at ends of ribbon.

6. Attach adhesive-backed magnet to back of large heart.

time-saving tip

A Stitch in Time

To save time, use a running stitch instead of the blanket stitch.

CHAPTER 3

Whether you're commuting for business or roaming the side streets and cafés of an old European city, bringing along small personal items always makes traveling more enjoyable. They are touchstones to what you left behind, a reminder of the comforts of home, and they also show a hint of your personal style to the new people you meet.

On the following pages you will find easy ideas to protect your valuables (and unmentionables), prepare you for fixing lost buttons and loose hems, and help you find your suitcase among a sea of luggage. Have fun getting ready for your next adventure while crafting the projects found in this chapter, including an elegant change purse, a simple jewelry pouch, a pretty passport holder, and a handy contact lens case.

Luggage Tag

Materials

- Button: ⅞"
- Chenille needle: size 20
- Copier
- Copier paper
- Craft glue
- Craft scissors
- Embroidery floss: brown, ivory
- Fabric marker pencil
- Heavyweight interfacing: 4" x 7"
- Ruler
- Straight pins
- Temporary spray adhesive
- Twine (10")
- Wool felt: brown, dark ivory

Instructions

Note: All stitching is done using six strands of embroidery floss, unless otherwise noted.

1. Photocopy Luggage Tag Template two times (page 119); cut out and pin to brown felt. Cut out shapes. Remove pins and templates.

2. Photocopy Interfacing Template (page 119); cut out and pin template to heavyweight interfacing. Cut out shape. Remove pins and templates.

3. Photocopy Business Card Pocket Template (page 119); cut out and pin to dark ivory felt. Cut out shape. Remove pins and template.

4. Using brown embroidery floss, stitch around perimeter of business card felt piece, ⅛" from edge, using primitive running stitch.

5. **To make pocket:** Apply thin line of glue near three edges of backside of business card felt piece and center, glue side down, on rectangular portion of tag front. Finger press in place.

6. Spray back of tag front and tag back with temporary spray adhesive. Sandwich heavyweight interfacing between tag front and back, matching all edges.

7. Using ivory embroidery floss, stitch layers together using buttonhole stitch around perimeter of tag. Tie off.

8. Securely sew button to angled edge of tag. Tie twine around button.

Change Purse

Materials

- Beads (4)
- Chenille needle: size 20
- Copier
- Copier paper
- Craft scissors
- Embroidery floss: dark red
- Fabric marker pencil
- Prong snaps (2)
- Straight pins
- Wool felt: dark gold, green

Instructions

Note: All stitching is done using six strands of embroidery floss.

1. Photocopy Change Purse Template (page 120) twice; cut out templates and pin one to dark gold felt and one to green felt. Cut out shapes. Remove pins and templates.

2. Photocopy Change Purse Pocket Template (page 120) twice; cut out templates and pin one to dark gold felt and one to green felt. Cut out shapes. Remove pins and templates.

3. Layer pieces: pocket, purse, purse, pocket, making sure to align edges. Pin in place. Using blanket stitch, sew layers together around pocket sides. Tie off.

4. Embellish flaps of change purse with beads sewn to outside and prong snaps to underside of flaps and front of flaps.

time-saving tip

Protect Your Pennies

To prevent change from slipping through the seams of the change purse, make sure your stitches are close together and securely sewn.

Jewelry Pouch

Materials

- Buttons (3)
- Chenille needle: size 22
- Copier
- Copier paper
- Craft scissors
- Embroidery floss: soft red
- Fabric glue
- Fabric marker pencil
- Felted wool: green, soft red
- Gingham ribbon: two coordinating colors (18")
- Iron
- Pressing cloth
- Ruler
- Safety pin: small
- Seam sealant
- Straight pins

Instructions

Note: All stitching is done using three strands of embroidery floss.

1. Cut two 3¾"x 6¼" rectangles from soft red felt.

2. Photocopy Jewelry Pouch Leaves Template (page 49) three times; cut out templates and pin to green felt. Cut out shapes. Remove pins and templates.

3. **To create flap:** Fold top 4"-wide edge of each rectangle down 1" and press with iron, using pressing cloth. Repeat on other felt piece.

4. **To create casing for ribbon ties:** Lift up flap and apply narrow line of fabric glue along inside cut edge of flap. Finger press flap to backside of pouch front. *Note:* This is the inside of pouch. Repeat on remaining felt piece.

time-saving tip

For Gift Giving

The jewelry pouch would make a wonderful gift. Craft a few ahead of time to make sure that you always have some on hand. Create them in a few different colors and use a variety of buttons.

Above: Simple ribbon pulls keep cherished jewels safely stored away for travel.

5. With casings of rectangles at top and matching all edges, place rectangles wrong sides together.

6. Leaving top of pouch open, and beginning and ending 1" down from top folded edge, buttonhole stitch down one side, across bottom and up second side, ending at bottom of casing. Tie off.

7. Apply seam sealant to raw edges of casing openings.

8. Center and glue three leaf shapes to pouch front.

9. Center buttons on leaf shapes and glue in place.

10. **To make gathering ties:** Attach safety pin to one end of ribbon and thread ribbon through pouch front casing and out through pouch back casing. Remove safety pin. *Note:* You now have two cut ribbon ends coming out of left side of pouch casing and two coming out of right side.

11. On left side of pouch, bring cut ends of ribbon together and tie into knot. Repeat on right side of pouch.

12. Cut ribbon ends at angle and apply seam sealant to ends.

Above: Seam sealant prevents fabric edges from fraying.

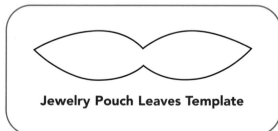

Jewelry Pouch Leaves Template

time-saving tip

Prevent Knotted Chains

To keep necklaces and earrings from getting tangled, make a separate jewelry pouch for each different type of jewelry, such as watches, earrings, necklaces, and bracelets.

Hosiery Envelope

Materials

- Button: 1" ivory
- Chenille needle: size 20
- Copier
- Copier paper
- Craft scissors
- Embroidery floss: ivory, soft red
- Fabric marker pencil
- Felted wool: dark ivory, light ivory, medium ivory, soft red
- Ruler
- Straight pins

Instructions

Note: All stitching is done using six strands of embroidery floss.

1. Cut one 10"x 6" rectangle (envelope front) and one 10"x 5" rectangle (envelope back) from soft red felt.

2. Photocopy Hosiery Envelope Pointed Flap Template (page 121); cut out template and pin to soft red felt. Cut out shape. Remove pins and template.

3. Photocopy Hosiery Leaves Template (page 121) twice; cut out templates and pin to medium ivory felt. Cut out shapes. Remove pins and templates.

4. Photocopy Large Hosiery Flower Template (page 121); cut out template and pin to light ivory felt. Cut out shape. Remove pins and template.

5. Photocopy Medium Hosiery Flower Template (page 121); cut out template and pin to medium ivory felt. Cut out shape. Remove pins and template.

6. Photocopy Small Hosiery Flower Template (page 121); cut out template and pin to dark ivory felt. Cut out shape. Remove pins and template.

7. Place small flower on medium flower to left of center, as shown.

8. Using soft red embroidery floss, stitch small flower to medium flower with primitive running stitch.

9. Place medium flower on large flower to left of center, as shown. Using soft red embroidery floss, stitch medium flower to large flower with primitive running stitch, and then stitch large flower to center of envelope.

Above: The felt interior of the hosiery envelope cradles delicate lingerie in softness and protects hosiery from pulls and runs.

Above: Two time-honored stitches, running and blanket stitches, make the hosiery pouch project perfect for beginning crafters.

10. Pin leaves to left and right sides of flower and buttonhole stitch leaves to envelope.

11. Using ivory embroidery floss, stitch primitive running stitch to top edge of envelope back, sides, and angled point of envelope flap.

12. Starting just below top edge of envelope back, buttonhole stitch envelope back to backside of envelope front. Continue buttonhole stitching up side of envelope front, making sure not to catch sides of pointed flap.

13. Buttonhole stitch top of pointed flap to envelope front and continue down side, making sure to catch pocket. Tie off.

14. Sew button close to pointed edge of envelope flap.

time-saving tip

No-Sew Appliqué

Apply fusible web to the backside of felted wool shapes. Stitch flowers together, and then iron to fuse flower and leaf shapes in place onto the envelope front.

Luggage Identifier

Materials

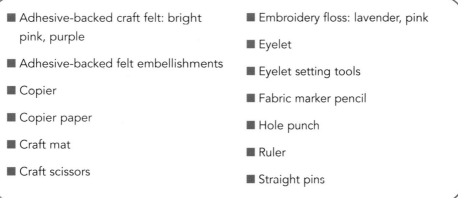

- Adhesive-backed craft felt: bright pink, purple
- Adhesive-backed felt embellishments
- Copier
- Copier paper
- Craft mat
- Craft scissors
- Embroidery floss: lavender, pink
- Eyelet
- Eyelet setting tools
- Fabric marker pencil
- Hole punch
- Ruler
- Straight pins

Instructions

1. Photocopy Luggage Identifier Template (page 122) twice; cut out templates and pin to purple felt. Cut out shapes. Remove pins and templates.

2. Photocopy Luggage Flower Template (page 122) twice, and Small Flower and Large Flower templates (page 123) once; cut out templates and pin one to pink felt and one to purple felt. Cut out shapes. Remove pins and templates.

3. Remove backing from circles, line up edges and finger press to secure.

4. Remove backing from flowers and wrap embroidery floss around each one to embellish. Center one flower on each side and finger press to secure.

5. Remove backing from felt embellishments, wrap embroidery floss around each one, and then layer on top of flowers.

6. Punch hole ½" inch from edge. Place luggage identifier on craft mat. Set eyelet in hole.

time-saving tip

Find Your Luggage

Make luggage identifiers in varying colors. Assign a color to each family member so he or she can easily claim his or her luggage, saving time searching for each case.

Sewing Kit

Materials

- Button with shank: ⅞"
- Chenille needle: size 22
- Copier
- Copier paper
- Craft scissors
- Embroidery floss: gold
- Fabric glue (optional)
- Fabric marker pencil
- Iron
- Pressing cloth
- Ruler
- Straight pins
- Wool felt: dark periwinkle blue, light gold, light periwinkle blue, medium gold

Instructions

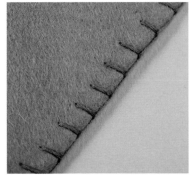

1. Cut one 4¾" x 8½" rectangle from dark periwinkle blue felt for cover.

2. From light periwinkle blue wool felt, cut one 4¼" x 7¾" rectangle for pages and one ¼" x 8" strip for tie closure.

3. Photocopy Small Flower Template (page 123); cut out template and pin to light gold felt. Cut out shape. Remove pins and template.

4. Photocopy Large Flower Template (page 123); cut out template and pin to medium gold felt. Cut out shape. Remove pins and template.

5. Stack and offset small flower on large flower.

6. Center and sew button on flower, making sure to sew through all layers. Set aside.

time-saving tip

Prepare For Emergencies

The felt pages of the sewing kit are designed to store buttons and pins as well as needles that are pre-threaded with your most-used colors.

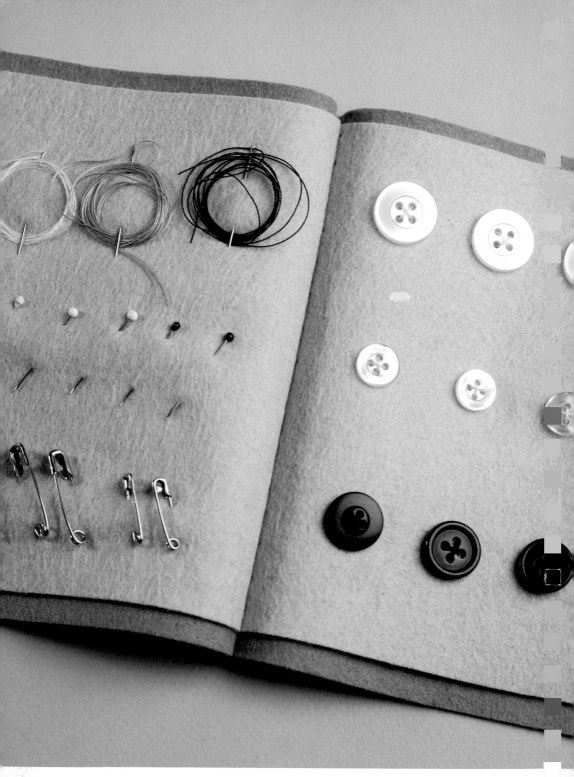

Above: Fill the felt pages of this little book with sewing necessities, including pre-threaded needles, pins, and a variety of buttons. Make sure to refill the pages before traveling.

Above: A shanked button provides a strong clasp for the felt closure on the sewing kit. Small pieces of projects, like the flowers and felt strip, can be made using felt scraps.

7. Set rectangle for cover on flat work surface. Center and stack rectangle for pages on top of cover.

8. Fold cover in half like a book and press with iron along crease, using pressing cloth. Repeat for pages. Open cover and center opened pages on top.

9. Hold folded cover, with the pages inside, in your lap with fold towards your waist.

10. **To bind cover:** Buttonhole stitch on folded edge, making sure to sew through all layers.

11. Center tie closure ¾" in from cut edge of inside back cover; sew or glue tie closure to back cover.

12. To securely close sewing kit, wrap tie closure around button shank.

time-saving tip

Add a Pair of Scissors

To make sure you have everything you need, tie a small pair of scissors to the end of the tie closure. Tuck the scissors inside of the pages for safety.

Passport Holder

Materials

- Buttons: ⅝" (2)
- Chenille needle: size 22
- Copier
- Copier paper
- Craft glue
- Craft scissors
- Embroidery floss: dusty blue, red
- Fabric glue
- Fabric marker pencil
- Felted wool: dusty blue, red
- Iron
- Pressing cloth
- Ruler
- Straight pins

Instructions

Note: All stitching is done with three strands of embroidery floss.

1. From red felted wool, cut one 5½" x 7¾" rectangle, one 2½" x 5½" rectangle, and two 2½" triangles.

2. Photocopy Car and Airplane templates (page 62); cut out templates and pin to dusty blue felt. Cut out shapes. Remove pins and templates.

3. Fold rectangle for passport in half (like a book) and arrange car and airplane shapes on passport front. Press with iron, using pressing cloth.

4. Apply dots of glue to back of car and airplane shapes and glue shapes in place.

5. Using dusty blue embroidery floss, buttonhole stitch around all cut edges of car and airplane. Glue buttons for car wheels in place.

time-saving tip

Use Different Wheels

Circles of brown felt could also be used for the car wheels. All you have to do is hole punch brown felt and glue circles in place to serve as wheels.

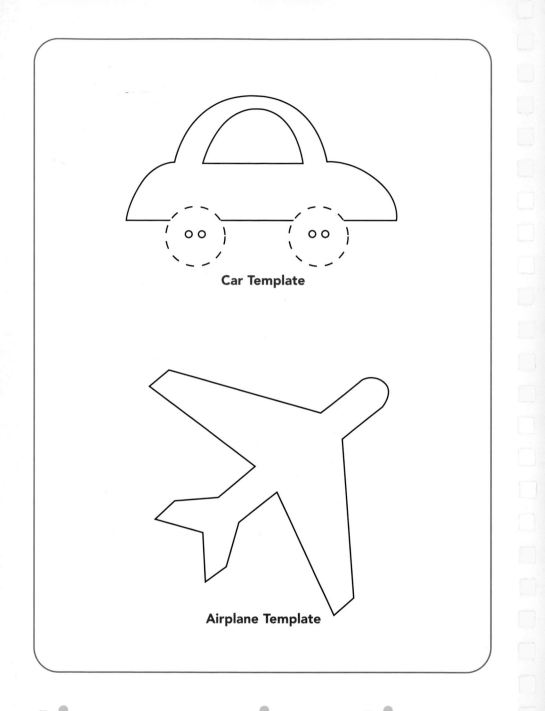

Car Template

Airplane Template

time-saving tip

Pucker-Free Projects

Iron cutouts to smooth out any puckers. Also, be sure to use a pressing cloth to avoid shiny marks.

Above: The wheels on the car started their journey as shanked buttons. The shanks were snipped off and then the buttons were glued in place.

6. Pin sleeve lining inside front of passport, matching top, bottom, and side edges.

7. Pin triangle sleeve linings inside back of passport, matching top, bottom, and side edges.

8. Using red embroidery floss and making sure to catch sleeve linings and triangle edges, stitch a primitive running stitch around perimeter of passport cover about ⅛" in from cut edge.

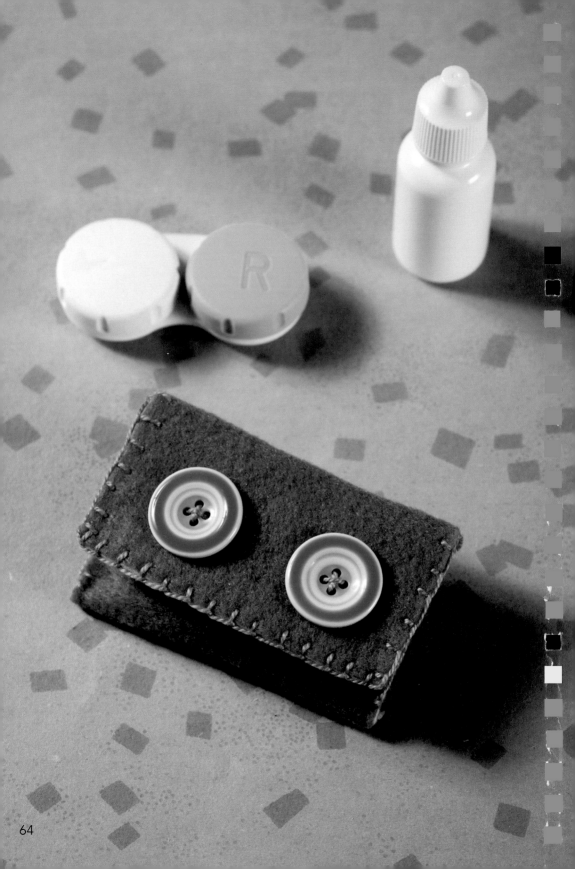

Contact Lens Case

Materials

- Buttons (2)
- Chenille needle: size 22
- Copier
- Copier paper
- Craft felt: light blue, white
- Craft scissors
- Embroidery floss: light blue
- Fabric marker pencil
- Ruler
- Sew-on snap
- Straight pins

Instructions

1. Cut one 7"x 3½" rectangle from light blue felt, and one from white felt.

2. Layer felt pieces, making sure to align edges. Fold bottom 3½" edge up 2". Pin pieces in place.

3. Lay felt down on flat surface. Mark evenly spaced holes, ⅛" apart and 1/16" from edge, down both sides and across the top. Using a blanket stitch, sew pieces together where marked.

4. Sew buttons on flap of case, and stitch sew-on snap to underside of flap and front of case.

time-saving tip

Make a Tougher Case

To make a more rigid case, replace the light blue craft felt with adhesive-backed craft felt.

CHAPTER 4

Your home is a reflection of your personality, ideas, and lifestyle. The things that surround you should celebrate who you are and what you enjoy. Handmade accessories make you feel at home in every room of your house, from the kitchen and dining room to the bedroom. The projects on these pages will help you beautify your rooms and create a warm, inviting atmosphere with elegant accessories made in your personal style. From a whimsical door hanger to a simple beaded picture frame and a lovely trinket box, the projects in this chapter will help transform your home into a personal haven. These clever ideas, including a vintage-inspired knitting needle holder, needle covers, and napkin rings, will show you easy ways to organize and embellish your spaces.

Door Hanger

Materials

- Adhesive-backed craft felt: green, pink, white
- Copier
- Copier paper
- Craft glue
- Fabric marker pencil
- Glass beads (2)
- Inkpad: green
- Scissors: craft, pinking shears
- Straight pins
- Toothpick
- Wool felt: green

Instructions

1. Photocopy Door Hanger Template (page 123) twice; cut out templates and pin one to white adhesive-backed craft felt and one to green wool felt. Cut out white felt with craft scissors and green wool felt with pinking shears. Remove pins and templates.

2. Photocopy Door Hanger Flower Template (page 123); cut out template and pin to pink adhesive-backed craft felt. Cut out shape. Remove pins and template.

3. Photocopy Door Hanger Leaves and Flower Pot templates (page 123); cut out templates and pin to green adhesive-backed craft felt. Cut out shapes. Remove pins and templates.

4. Remove backing from white felt, position over green wool felt, and finger press to secure. This is the back of the door hanger. Place door hanger, right side up, on flat surface. Using inkpad, color toothpick. Insert toothpick as stem for flower. Set aside.

5. Starting ½" from bottom of door hanger, position pieces as shown. Remove backing from felt pieces and finger press in place. Glue glass beads to center of flower.

time-saving tip

Write It Out

Instead of using suggested embellishments, use ready-made adhesive-backed felt letters to spell out sayings such as "Baby's Sleeping" or "Do Not Disturb."

Picture Frame

Materials

- Beads: small pink
- Craft scissors
- Double-sided tape: extra tacky
- Embroidery floss: white
- Fabric marker pencil
- Photograph
- Ruler
- Wool felt: heavyweight pink

Instructions

1. Cut two 5" square pieces of felt, and then cut 2" square from center of one piece. Cut two 1¼" x 4¼" pieces of felt.

2. Using blanket stitch, stitch 5" square pieces together, leaving 2½" opening at top.

3. Using running stitch, sew two 1¼" x 4¼" pieces of felt together. This is frame stand. Stitch top of frame stand to the back of frame, ½" from top.

4. Adhere double-sided tape around cutout in front of frame. Press small beads into tape to secure. Insert photograph in frame.

time-saving tip

For Extra Strength

To ensure that the frame sits straight, insert a 4½" length of heavy-duty craft wire up the center of the two layers of the frame stand.

Photo Envelope

Materials

- Buttons (3)
- Chenille needle: size 20
- Copier
- Copier paper
- Embroidery floss: green, pink, yellow
- Fabric marker pencil
- Felted wool: gold, green, red
- Flower embellishment: white
- Iron
- Pressing cloth
- Ribbon: ⅜"-wide silk (16")
- Scissors: craft, pinking shears
- Straight pins

Instructions

1. Using pinking shears, cut one 9½" x 6⅝" rectangle from red felt.

2. Using craft scissors, cut two 6½" x 3" rectangles from gold felt.

3. Photocopy Large Paisley Template (page 75) three times; cut out templates and pin to gold felt. Cut out shapes using pinking shears. Remove pins and templates.

4. Photocopy Small Paisley Template (page 75) three times; cut out templates and pin to green felt. Cut out shapes using pinking shears. Remove pins and templates.

5. Using craft scissors, cut out centers of small paisleys. Stitch small paisleys to large paisleys with yellow embroidery floss and large paisleys to red rectangle with red embroidery floss, as shown; sew on buttons.

6. Fold red rectangle in half and press with iron, using pressing cloth.

time-saving tip

Be Prepared

Make a photo envelope for each type of satchel you carry—your purse, briefcase, or computer case—that way you will always have photographs on hand to share.

Above: Open the photo envelope to reveal two generous pockets that easily hold favorite photographs.

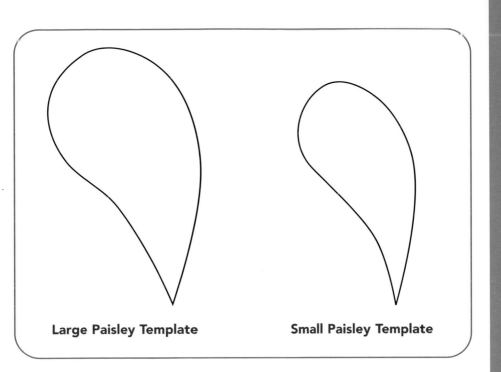

Large Paisley Template   **Small Paisley Template**

7. Pin gold rectangles to inside of red felt rectangle. Using green embroidery floss, chain stitch around red rectangle.

8. Cut ribbon into two 8" lengths. Attach one length to bottom center of middle paisley, tucking end under edge of paisley. Stitch remaining length of ribbon to bottom middle of inside square with yellow embroidery floss, and then stitch flower embellishment over end of ribbon.

9. Close holder and tie ribbons together.

time-saving tip
Adhering Buttons
To save time, glue buttons to photo holder instead of stitching them to the paisleys.

Trinket Box

Materials

- Cardstock: heavyweight
- Chenille needle: size 22
- Copier
- Copier paper
- Craft scissors
- Embroidery floss: dusty rose, gold
- Fabric glue
- Fabric marker pencil
- Ruler
- Straight pins
- Wool felt: dark red, dusty rose, gold, strawberry red

Instructions

Note: All stitching is done using three strands of embroidery floss, unless noted.

1. Photocopy Trinket Box Template (page 78) four times; cut out templates and pin two to dusty rose felt and two to gold felt. Cut out shapes. Remove pins and templates.

2. Photocopy Square Template (page 78); cut out template and pin to dusty rose felt. Cut out shape. Remove pins and template.

3. Cut one 13½" x 3" strip of dusty rose felt and one strip from gold felt.

4. Photocopy Large Flower Template (page 123) twice; cut out templates and pin one to dark red felt and one to strawberry red felt. Cut out shapes. Remove pins and templates.

5. Photocopy Small Flower Template (page 123) twice; cut out templates and pin one to dark red felt and one to strawberry red felt. Cut out shapes. Remove pins and templates.

6. Photocopy Cardboard Insert Template twice (page 78); cut out templates and trace shapes onto heavyweight cardstock. Cut out shapes.

7. **To make layered flower:** Stack and offset large strawberry red flower on top of large dark red flower.

8. Stack and offset small dark red flower on top of large flowers. Stack and offset small strawberry red flower on top of small and large flowers. Stack dusty-rose square flower center on top of flower.

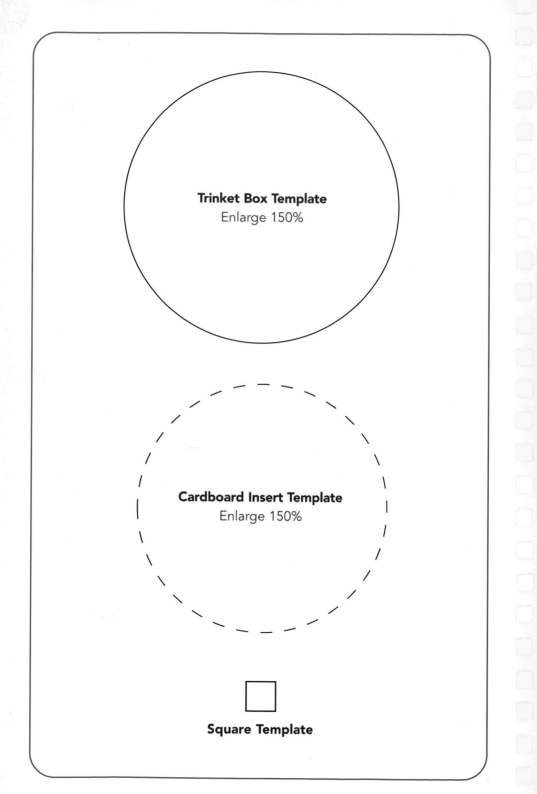

Trinket Box Template
Enlarge 150%

Cardboard Insert Template
Enlarge 150%

Square Template

9. Using gold embroidery floss, push chenille needle up through center of all flower layers and square. Make a French knot in center of square.

10. Push needle back down through all flower layers and tie off floss on back of layered flower. Set aside.

11. To make trinket box bottom, stack gold circle on top of dusty rose circle.

12. Using dusty rose embroidery floss, buttonhole stitch around half of circle and place cardstock insert between two circles, then continue buttonhole stitching around perimeter of circles. If needed, trim cardboard to size.

13. Repeat Steps 11 and 12 for top of trinket box. Glue flower to center of gold circle for top of trinket box.

14. Place finished trinket box circle (designated for the trinket box bottom), dusty rose side up, on flat work surface.

15. Matching all sides, place strips for sides of trinket box together vertically on top of trinket box bottom, making sure that dusty rose strip is inside. Match the strips to exact size of circle. *Note:* Strips will overlap.

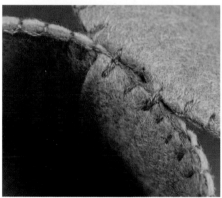

Top: Offset layers are the secret to creating the pretty flower embellishment. Fabric glue holds the layers together. **Above:** Cardstock inserts strengthen the sides of the trinket box. The hinge is created with a few simple straight stitches.

16. **To make sides of trinket box:** Carefully glue ends of strips together. Using dusty-rose embroidery floss, buttonhole stitch around perimotor of top and bottom of glued strips. *Note:* The sides of the trinket box are now complete.

17. **To begin forming trinket box:** Use one strand of dusty-rose embroidery floss and sew bottom circle to sides, with lining sides together.

18. **To make a hinge:** Use dusty-rose embroidery floss to sew two stitches at back of trinket box, to left and right sides of back seam, to connect top to sides. The top should open and close easily.

Napkin Ring

Materials

- Craft scissors
- Fabric glue
- Fabric marker pencil
- Ruler
- Straight pins
- Wool felt: dark periwinkle blue, gold, light periwinkle blue

Instructions

1. Cut two 1" x 6" strips from gold felt.

2. Photocopy Square Flower Center Template (page 124) twice; cut out templates and pin to gold felt. Cut out shapes. Remove pins and templates.

3. Photocopy Napkin Ring Large Flower and Napkin Ring Small Flower templates (page 124) twice; cut out templates and pin one of each to dark periwinkle blue felt and one of each to light periwinkle blue felt. Cut out shapes. Remove pins and templates.

4. **To make ring:** Loop 1" x 6" strip into circle, overlapping cut ends by ½".

5. Carefully apply dots of glue in overlapped area of strip and finger press ends together. Set aside.

6. Place small dot of glue on back of small flower. Alternating colors, center and stack small flower, glue side down, on top of large flower and finger press.

7. Place small dot of glue on square flower center. Center square, glue side down, on small flower and finger press. *Note: Flower is completed.*

8. Place glue on backside of completed flower. Center flower on overlapped area of napkin ring, glue side down, and finger press in place.

time-saving tip

Add Some Sparkle

Glamorize your table setting by simply gluing rhinestones to the center of the flower on the napkin ring.

Receipt Holder

Materials

- Beads: small (3)
- Copier
- Copier paper
- Craft knife
- Craft mat
- Craft scissors
- Embroidery floss: bright pink
- Fabric marking pencil
- Felted wool: dark green, dark pink, light green, light pink, purple
- Hole punch
- Ruler
- Self-adhesive craft felt: bright pink
- Self-adhesive hook-and-loop dot
- Straight pins

Instructions

1. Photocopy Small Leaf Template (page 85) twice; cut out templates and pin to dark green felt. Cut out shapes.

2. Photocopy Small Circle Template (page 85) three times; cut out templates and pin one to dark pink felt, one to light pink felt, and one to purple felt. Cut out shapes.

3. Cut one 6"x 8" piece of bright pink felt and one same size piece from green felt.

4. Fold bottom 6" edge up 2½". Fold top 6" edge down 2". Finger press to mark seams. Using blanket stitch, sew leaf shapes to top flap; layer and then sew circles onto leaf shapes. Sew bead onto each circle.

5. Remove backing from bright pink felt; line up edges with green felt and finger press pieces together to secure.

time-saving tip

Infuse a Little Elegance

Stitch beads at each hole as you stitch around the perimeter of the receipt holder to quickly add a touch of elegance.

Above: This pretty pouch helps keep receipts organized, while the hook-and-loop closure keeps them safely tucked inside.

Above: Small beads sewn in the center of diminuitive felt flowers serve as the stamens, as well as add a bit of color and detail.

6. Mark twenty evenly spaced holes down each side, ⅛" in from edge. Punch hole at each mark. Fold up bottom edge at original seam.

7. Stitch around perimeter, creating pocket. Tie off.

8. Mark placement on flap and pocket for self-adhesive hook-and-loop dot. Place dots on marks then secure with a couple of stitches around edges of each dot. Close flap.

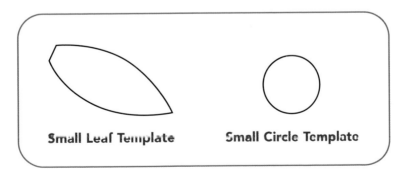

Small Leaf Template   **Small Circle Template**

time-saving tip

Removing Pencil Marks

Removing pencil marks from felt is easy. Simply mix a tiny bit of bleach-free detergent into a bowl of cool water, and dip a cotton swab in the water. Gently rub marks with moist swab until mark is gone.

Knitting Needle Holder

Materials

- Chenille needle: size 22
- Craft scissors
- Embroidery floss: ivory
- Fabric marker pencil
- Gingham ribbon: 1½"-wide green-and-ivory (1 yard)
- Ruler
- Seam sealant
- Straight pins
- Wool felt: 36"-wide green (½ yard)

Instructions

Note: All stitching is done using three strands of floss.

1. Cut one 17"x 15" rectangle from felt for needle holder, one 17"x 9" rectangle for pocket, and one 17"x 4" rectangle for flap.

2. Cut ends of ribbon into "V" shape and apply seam sealant to ends. Fold ribbon in half. Set aside.

3. Stitch primitive running stitch ⅛" in from cut edge for top of needle pocket and side and bottom edges of flap.

4. Pin pocket to needle holder, matching side and bottom edges. Sandwich and pin folded edge of ribbon ½" between right top edge of pocket and needle holder. Pin flap to top edge of needle holder.

5. Starting just below ribbon, buttonhole stitch pocket to needle holder. Continue buttonhole stitching up side of needle holder, making sure not to catch sides of flap. Buttonhole stitch top of flap to needle holder and continue down side, making sure to catch ribbon. Tie off.

6. **To make slots for knitting needles:** Start at left side of pocket, just inside buttonhole stitching, and use ruler and fabric marker pencil to draw ten vertical lines 1½" apart from top of pocket to bottom.

7. Using embroidery floss, stitch primitive running stitch directly on top of lines drawn in Step 6.

Needle Covers

Materials

- Chenille needle: size 22
- Craft punch: small circle
- Craft scissors
- Elastic cord: black
- Embroidery floss: dark blue, dark red, tan
- Fabric marker pencil
- Ruler
- Straight pins
- Wool felt: brown, dark blue, dark red, green, light blue, light rose, orange, yellow

Instructions

Note: All stitching is done using one strand of embroidery floss.

1. Photocopy Needle Cover Template (page 124) four times; cut out templates and pin one to dark blue felt, one to dark red felt, one to light blue felt, and one to light rose felt. Cut out shapes. Remove pins and templates.

2. Using craft punch, punch small circles from all colors of felt. Using tan embroidery floss and French knot technique, attach seven punched felt pieces in a flower shape to light blue needle cover and light rose needle cover, and then add three French knots.

3. Pin light blue needle cover to dark blue needle cover and light rose needle cover to dark red needle cover. Using blanket stitch, stitch both sets of needle covers using coordinating embroidery floss.

4. Stuff tips of needle covers with excess felt. Attach one end of black elastic cord to each needle cover.

time-saving tip

Fast Gift Idea

The needle covers are fun and fast to make. They also would be great ornaments or gift embellishments.

CHAPTER 5

Handmade gifts from the heart are a sure way to let someone know how much you care. Create felted accessories to thank friends and family for the little things they do every day like listening when we need to share, helping with carpools and play dates, and encouraging us to laugh.

Make a welcome entrance by presenting your hostess with a gift of pretty coasters, celebrate a new home with a beautiful room sachet, dress up a simple gift card with a charming gift card cover, and honor a friend's love of literature with a pretty book cover.

The projects featured in this chapter, from a cheery notepad holder to a cell phone cover embellished with buttons, will tell special friends just how much they mean to you.

Cell Phone Cover

Materials

- Beading thread
- Buttons: mother-of-pearl donuts (13)
- Craft glue
- Craft scissors
- Embroidery floss: light yellow
- Ribbon: 1"-wide (15")
- Ruler
- Wool felt: green

Instructions

Note: All stitching is done using six strands of embroidery floss.

1. From green felt, cut two 3" x 4½" rectangles and one 1½" x 12" strip.

2. Using blanket stitch and embroidery floss, stitch pieces together, as shown.

3. Using beading thread, string twelve donut buttons together. Knot each end of thread and secure with dot of glue.

4. Cut ribbon to 10" length and 5" length. Weave 10" of ribbon through beads, leaving 1" tail at each end. Secure two buttons at each end to either top side of cell phone case.

5. Tie 5" length to remaining donut button. Secure to front of cell phone case with craft glue.

time-saving tip

Hold the Buttons

To save time, just use pretty ribbon for the handle and case front, and forgo the addition of buttons.

Gift Tag

Materials

- Chenille needle: size 22
- Copier
- Copier paper
- Embroidery floss: brown, dark rose, green, ivory, light rose
- Fabric glue
- Felted wool: brown, dark rose, ivory, green, light rose
- Heavyweight interfacing: 4" x 7"
- Hole punch
- Ribbon (10")
- Scissors: craft, pinking shears
- Straight pins
- Temporary spray adhesive

Instructions

Note: All stitching is done with three strands of embroidery floss.

1. Photocopy Gift Tag Template (page 96) twice; cut out templates and pin to ivory felt. Cut out shapes with pinking shears. Remove pins and templates.

2. Photocopy Interfacing Template (page 96); cut out template and pin to heavy-weight interfacing. Cut out with craft scissors. Remove pins and template.

3. Photocopy Large Tag Flower Template (page 96); cut out template and pin to dark rose felt. Cut out shape with craft scissors. Remove pins and templates.

4. Photocopy Small Tag Flower Template (page 96); cut out template and pin to light rose felt. Cut out shape with craft scissors. Remove pins and templates.

5. Photocopy Leaf Template (page 96) four times; cut out templates and pin to green felt. Cut out shapes with craft scissors. Remove pins and templates.

time-saving tip

Make A No-Sew Gift Tag

Instead of stitching the gift tag, use fusible web between the layers and to adhere embellishments.

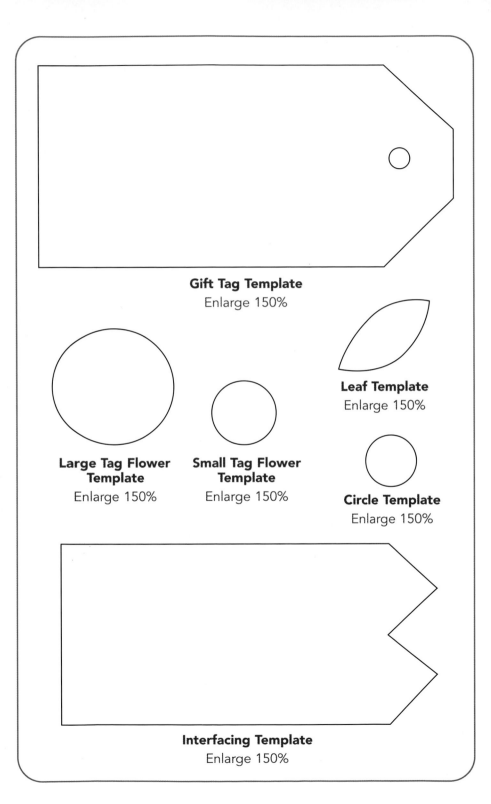

Gift Tag Template
Enlarge 150%

Leaf Template
Enlarge 150%

**Large Tag Flower
Template**
Enlarge 150%

**Small Tag Flower
Template**
Enlarge 150%

Circle Template
Enlarge 150%

Interfacing Template
Enlarge 150%

Above: To personalize the gift tag, either use adhesive-backed letters to spell out the recipient's name on the back of the tag, or pin a hand-written note to the back.

6. Photocopy Circle Template (page 96) twice; cut out templates and pin to brown felt. Cut out shapes. Remove pins and templates.

7. Align tag front to tag back and punch hole at angled end of tag. Punch hole in center of each circle, position around hole on front of tag and then stitch in place.

8. Arrange and glue flower and leaf shapes to tag front. Buttonhole stitch around perimeter of all shapes.

9. Spray back of tag front and tag back with temporary spray adhesive and then sandwich heavyweight interfacing between the two pieces, matching all edges.

10. Sew a primitive running stitch through all layers around perimeter of gift tag, ⅛" from cut edge. Tie off. Thread ribbon through hole for fastening tag to gift.

time-saving tip

Making Plenty

The gift tag is perfect for any occasion. Use red or green felt for the holidays, or pink or blue for a baby gift. If you make several beforehand, embellishing can be done in minutes.

Book Cover

Materials

- Chenille needle: size 20
- Copier
- Copier paper
- Craft scissors
- Embroidery floss: black
- Fabric glue
- Fabric marker pencil
- Fusible web
- Gingham ribbon: ⅜"-wide (2 yards)
- Ruler
- Straight pins
- Wool felt: black, dusty rose

Instructions

Note: All stitching is done using six strands of embroidery floss.

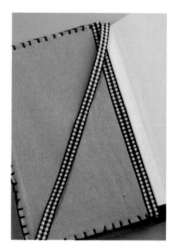

1. Photocopy Fleur-de-Lis Template (page 101); cut out template and pin to black felt. Cut out shape. Remove pins and template.

2. Measure front, spine, and back of book to be covered. Add ½" to height and ½" to length. (This will allow for a ¼"-wide buttonhole stitch around perimeter of cover.) Cut one rectangle for book cover from dusty rose felt.

3. Measure book front, adding ½" to height and subtracting 2" from width of measurement. Using this measurement, cut two rectangles for front and back flaps from dusty rose felt.

4. Determine length of ribbon bookmark by measuring height of book and adding 3". Cut ribbon for bookmark.

time-saving tip

Adding Embellishments

Glue a variety of buttons around the edges of the book cover for a fast and pretty embellishment.

Above: Felted panels protect the inside book covers and an attached bookmark is ready to be put to use.

5. Fold large dusty rose rectangle in half, like a book, and arrange fleur-de-lis shape on front cover. Carefully place 6" length of gingham ribbon under the fleur-de-lis, as shown, and stitch using one strand of embroidery floss. *Note:* You can also glue the cutout in place.

6. Finish by tying knot in ribbon and trimming ends to size.

7. To embellish flaps, glue gingham ribbon to inside edge of flap and trim to size. Repeat for second flap.

8. **To position bookmark:** Fold rectangle for book front, spine, and back cover in half and finger press to mark. Then unfold rectangle and place flat on work surface.

Fleur-de-Lis Template
Enlarge 150%

9. Glue one length of ribbon for bookmark, centered on inside spine, ½" down from top cut edge of spine. *Note:* Ribbon should extend at least 3" past book height.

10. To make sleeves for book cover, pin flaps to left and right sides of rectangle, matching top, side, and bottom edges.

11. Using six strands of embroidery floss and making sure to catch flaps and ribbon bookmark, buttonhole stitch around perimeter of book cover.

time-saving tip
Cut Out a Step
This book cover would be just as appealing without the ribbon bookmark. To save time, omit that step and consider inserting a store-bought bookmark.

Gift Card Holder

Materials

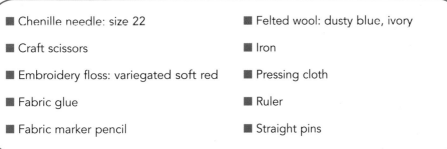

- Chenille needle: size 22
- Craft scissors
- Embroidery floss: variegated soft red
- Fabric glue
- Fabric marker pencil

- Felted wool: dusty blue, ivory
- Iron
- Pressing cloth
- Ruler
- Straight pins

Instructions

Note: All stitching is done using three strands of embroidery floss.

1. Photocopy Gift Card Holder Template (page 124) and Pocket Template (page 125); cut out templates and pin to dusty blue felt. Cut out shapes. Remove pins and templates.

2. Photocopy Gift Card Heart Template (page 124); cut out template and pin to ivory felt. Cut out shape. Remove pins and template.

3. Fold gift card holder in half along 4" side. Press lightly with iron, using pressing cloth.

4. Open gift card holder and align pocket with bottom and right side edges of inside back cover of gift card holder. Place narrow line of glue on seam line along side and bottom edges of pocket. Finger press pocket in place to secure glue.

5. Sew a primitive running stitch ⅛" in from cut edge around perimeter of gift card holder.

6. Center heart on front of gift card holder. Sew primitive running stitch ⅛" in from cut edge around perimeter of heart.

time-saving tip

Pick a Theme

Embellish the front of the gift card holder with a charm to represent the occasion, such as a cake for a birthday gift or a diaper pin for a baby gift.

Compact Mirror Sleeve

Materials

- Beading needle
- Beading thread
- Craft scissors
- Fabric glue
- Glass beads: small round (6), small faceted (4)
- Straight pins
- Wool felt: green

Instructions

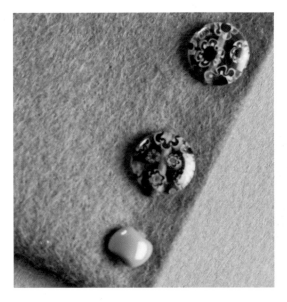

1. From green felt, cut one 4" x 7" rectangle.

2. Fold short edges in ½" and secure with dots of fabric glue.

3. Fold bottom short end up to top and pin in place.

4. Knot end of thread and string on faceted bead. Weave needle down one side, adding beads as you go. End with small faceted bead. Tie off. Repeat on other side.

time-saving tip

Sized to Fit

The mirror case can be made to fit any size mirror. Simply measure your mirror and add 1" to all sides. Proceed as above.

Sachet

Materials

- Chenille needle: size 20
- Copier
- Copier paper
- Craft scissors
- Embroidery floss: medium ivory, soft red
- Fabric glue
- Fabric marker pencil
- Felted wool: medium ivory, soft red
- Flower trim (6")
- Potpourri
- Straight pins

Instructions

Note: All stitching is done using six strands of embroidery floss.

1. Photocopy Sachet Square Template (page 125) twice; cut out templates and pin to soft red felt. Cut out shapes. Remove pins and templates.

2. Photocopy Sachet Heart Template (page 125); cut out template and pin to medium ivory felt. Cut out shape. Remove pins and template.

3. Place flower trim on front of heart shape. Carefully glue trim to heart, making sure to wrap excess trim to backside of heart and securing ends of trim with small amount of glue.

4. Center heart shape on one of the squares and secure in place with small dots of glue. Stitching close to cut edge of heart, sew heart to square with primitive running stitch using soft red embroidery floss.

5. Stack squares, wrong sides together, and make sure all edges match. Buttonhole stitch squares together around three sides using medium ivory embroidery floss. Fill sachet with potpourri and continue buttonhole stitching opening closed.

time-saving tip
Easy Filling Option

Instead of potpourri, use aroma beads (widely available at craft stores) to fill the sachet. Use a funnel to transfer the beads to the sachet, then buttonhole stitch the sachet closed.

Coaster Set

Materials

- Chenille needle: size 22
- Copier
- Copier paper
- Embroidery floss: light periwinkle blue, ivory
- Fabric glue
- Fabric marker pencil
- Scissors: craft, pinking shears
- Straight pins
- Wool felt: dark periwinkle blue, gold, green, light periwinkle blue

Instructions

Note: All stitching is done using three strands of embroidery floss.

1. Photocopy Large Coaster Circle Template (page 110) twice; cut out templates and pin to dark periwinkle felt. Cut out shapes with pinking shears. Remove pins and templates.

2. Photocopy Small Coaster Circles Template (page 110) twice; cut out templates and pin to gold felt. Cut out shapes with pinking shears. Remove pins and templates.

3. Photocopy Coaster Flower Template (page 110) twice; cut out templates and pin to light periwinkle blue felt. Cut out shapes with craft scissors. Remove pins and templates.

4. Photocopy Coaster Leaf Template (page 110) twice; cut out templates and pin to green felt. Cut out shapes with craft scissors. Remove pins and templates.

time-saving tip

Go with Faux
Rather than felt leaves, consider using millinery leaves for added interest. Simply adhere using fabric glue.

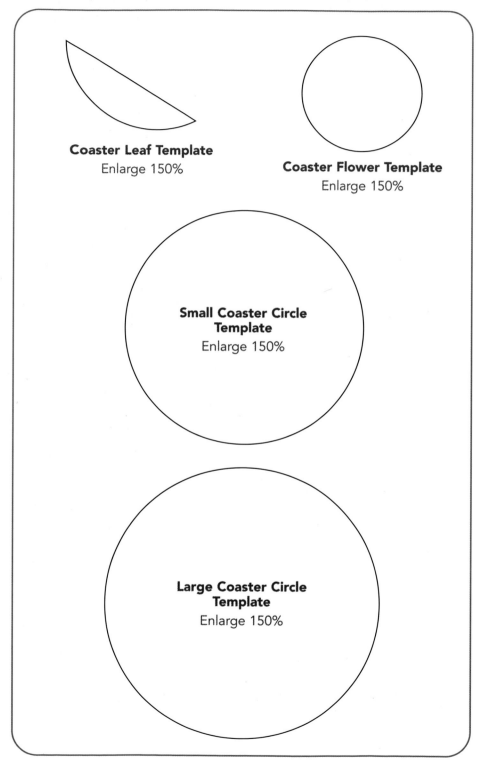

Coaster Leaf Template
Enlarge 150%

Coaster Flower Template
Enlarge 150%

Small Coaster Circle Template
Enlarge 150%

Large Coaster Circle Template
Enlarge 150%

Above: Using two layers of felt gives the coasters a firm foundation.

5. Arrange flower and leaf shapes on small circle and secure with dots of glue.

6. Buttonhole stitch around perimeter of flower with light periwinkle blue embroidery floss and leaf cutouts with ivory embroidery floss.

7. Center small circle onto large circle and secure with dots of glue.

8. Stitching close to cut edge of small circle, sew small circle to large circle with a primitive running stitch using light periwinkle blue embroidery floss. Repeat Steps 5-8 for second coaster.

time-saving tip

A Stiff Alternative

If you prefer a more firm set of coasters, consider cutting a round cardboard circle and inserting it between the two felt layers before stitching edges closed.

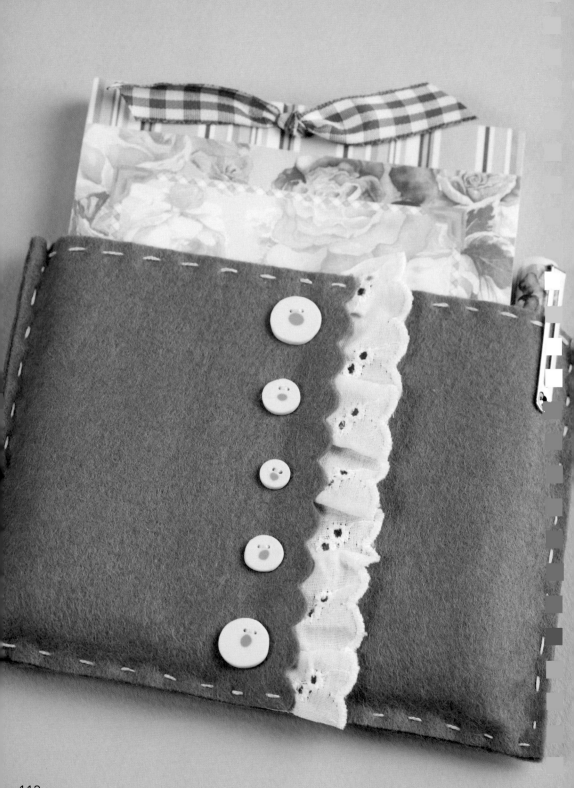

Notepad Holder

Materials

- Buttons: ¼"–½" (5)
- Chenille needle: size 22
- Embroidery floss: ivory
- Eyelet lace: 1"-wide (5")
- Fabric glue
- Ruler
- Scissors: craft, decorative-edge
- Straight pins
- Wool felt: blue

Instructions

Note: All stitching is done using six strands of embroidery floss.

1. From blue felt, cut one 4¾"x 6¼" rectangle for back and one 4¾"x 3½" rectangle for left front flap. Trim each 4¾" edge with decorative-edge scissors. Cut one 4¾"x 4" rectangle for right front flap.

2. Place narrow line of glue along back of decorative edge of left front flap. Position and finger press eyelet lace in place, as shown.

3. Arrange and sew or glue five buttons to left of decorative edge.

4. Lay notepad holder back on flat work surface.

5. Lay right front flap directly on top of back, aligning top, right side, and bottom edges.

6. Lay left front flap directly on top of back, aligning top, right side, and bottom edges and overlapping right front flap approximately 1".

time-saving tip

Make It Fit

Custom sizing the notepad holder is easy. Simply measure width, height, and depth of notepad and add ½" to top and one side of back. For front, flaps overlap by 1", and height and width equal size of rectangle for the back of the notepad.

Above: The simplest of stitches, a primitive running stitch, is used to sew around the edges of the notepad holder.

Above: To save time, the lace embellishment is glued into place.

7. In overlapped area, glue left and right flaps together. *Note:* The glued flaps now compose the front of the holder. The size of the front should exactly match the back of the notepad holder.

8. Stitch primitive running stitch along top edge of front and back rectangles of notepad holder, ⅛" in from cut edge.

9. Making sure all edges match and with wrong sides together, stack notepad holder front on notepad holder back.

10. Leaving top of notepad holder open, sew a primitive running stitch ⅛" in from cut edges for sides and bottom.

time-saving tip

Add Room For Accessories

If you would like to keep a pen or pencil next to the notepad, simply add their measurement to the ones you take for your notepad and adjust accordingly.

Templates

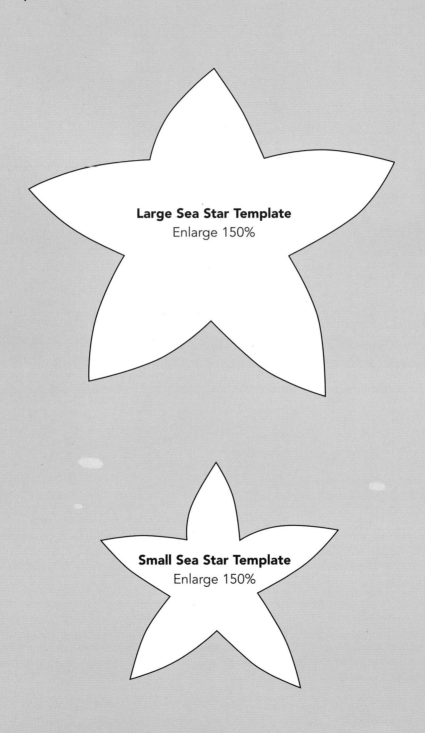

Large Sea Star Template
Enlarge 150%

Small Sea Star Template
Enlarge 150%

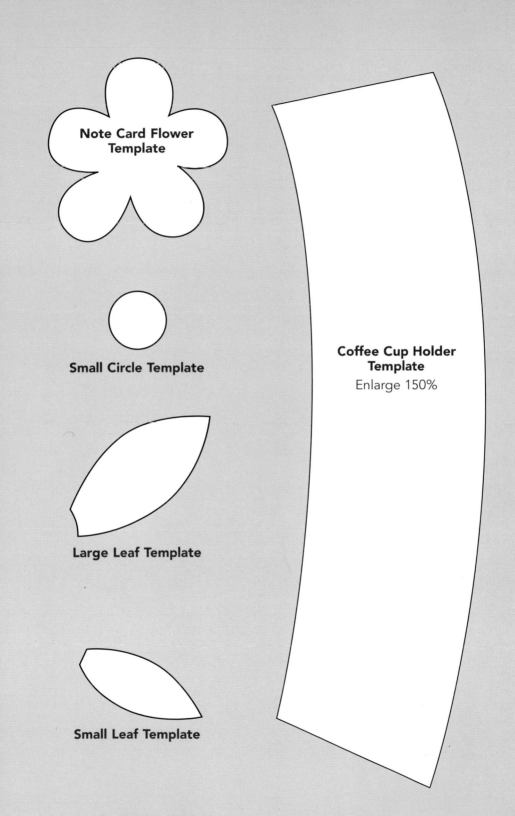

Note Card Flower Template

Small Circle Template

Large Leaf Template

Small Leaf Template

Coffee Cup Holder Template
Enlarge 150%

Templates

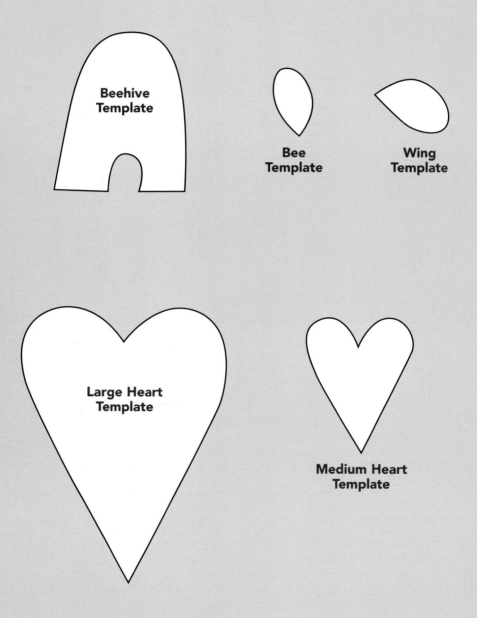

Beehive Template

Bee Template

Wing Template

Large Heart Template

Medium Heart Template

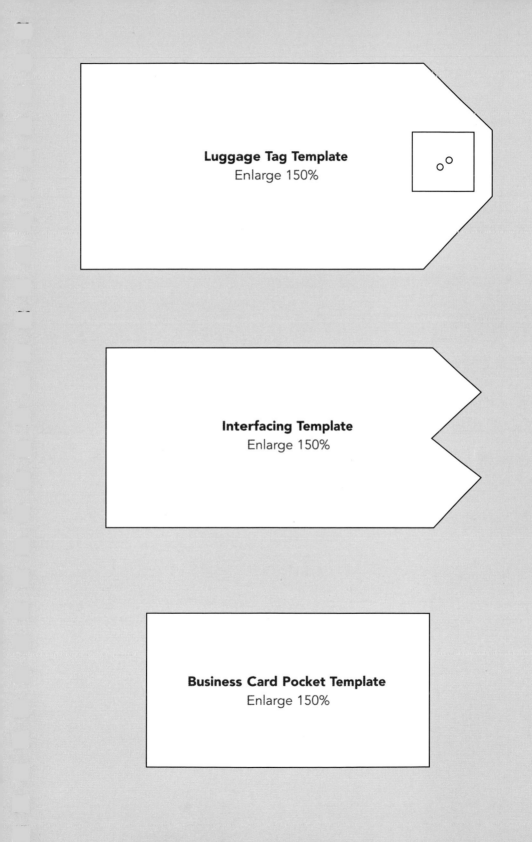

Luggage Tag Template
Enlarge 150%

Interfacing Template
Enlarge 150%

Business Card Pocket Template
Enlarge 150%

Templates

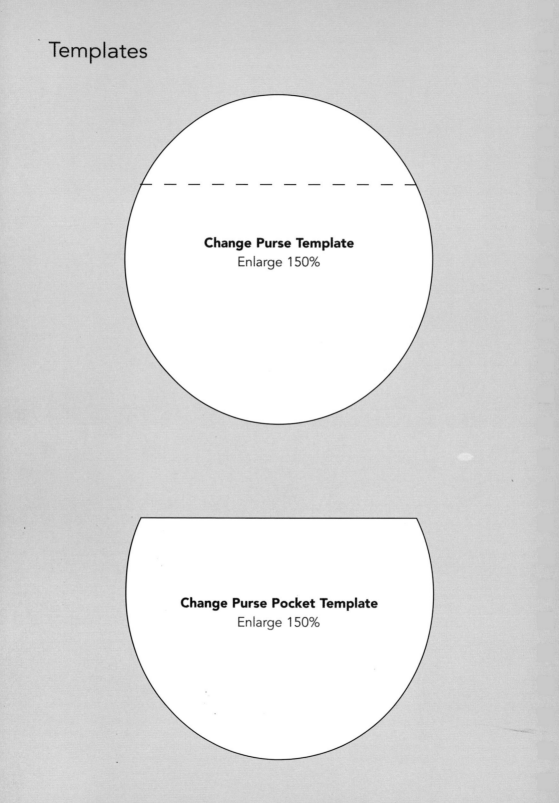

Change Purse Template
Enlarge 150%

Change Purse Pocket Template
Enlarge 150%

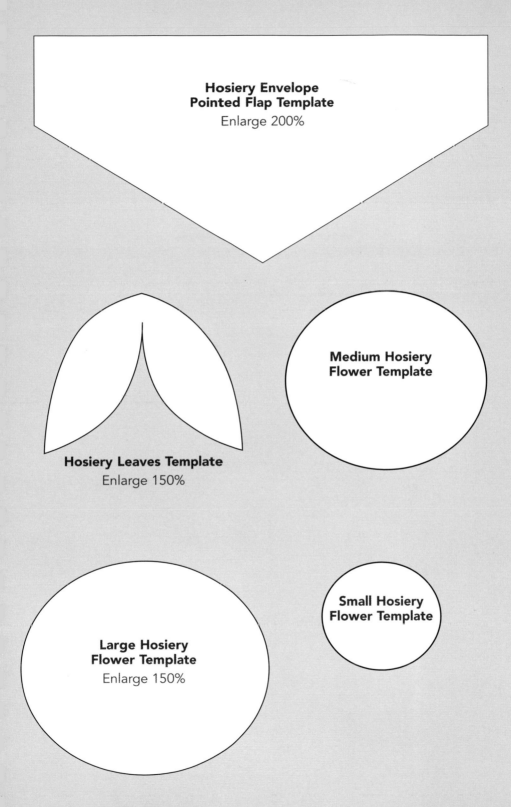

**Hosiery Envelope
Pointed Flap Template**
Enlarge 200%

**Medium Hosiery
Flower Template**

Hosiery Leaves Template
Enlarge 150%

**Large Hosiery
Flower Template**
Enlarge 150%

**Small Hosiery
Flower Template**

Templates

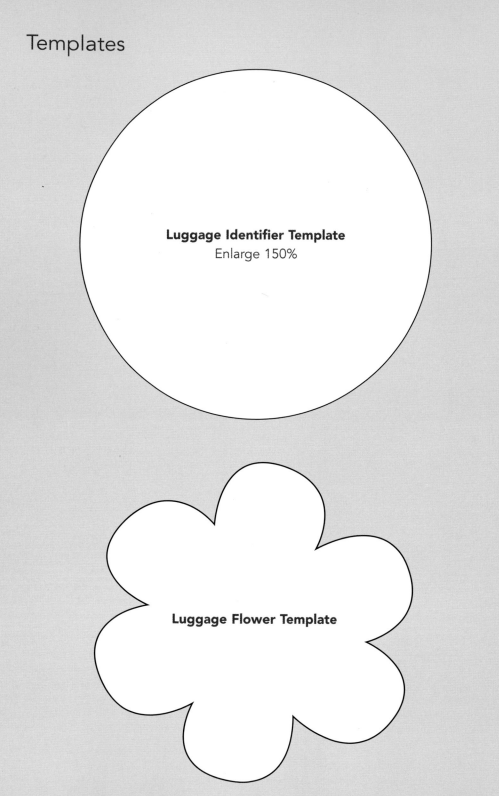

Luggage Identifier Template
Enlarge 150%

Luggage Flower Template

Small Flower Template
Enlarge 150%

Large Flower Template
Enlarge 150%

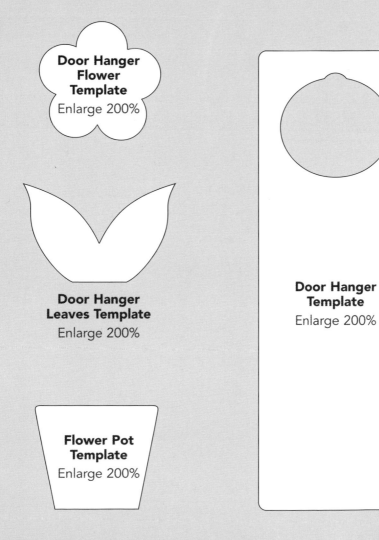

Door Hanger Flower Template
Enlarge 200%

Door Hanger Leaves Template
Enlarge 200%

Door Hanger Template
Enlarge 200%

Flower Pot Template
Enlarge 200%

Templates

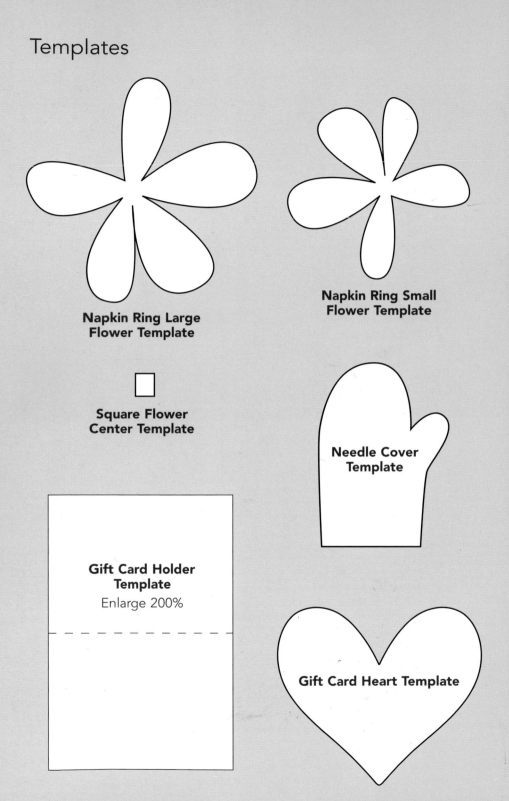

**Napkin Ring Large
Flower Template**

**Napkin Ring Small
Flower Template**

**Square Flower
Center Template**

**Needle Cover
Template**

**Gift Card Holder
Template**

Enlarge 200%

Gift Card Heart Template

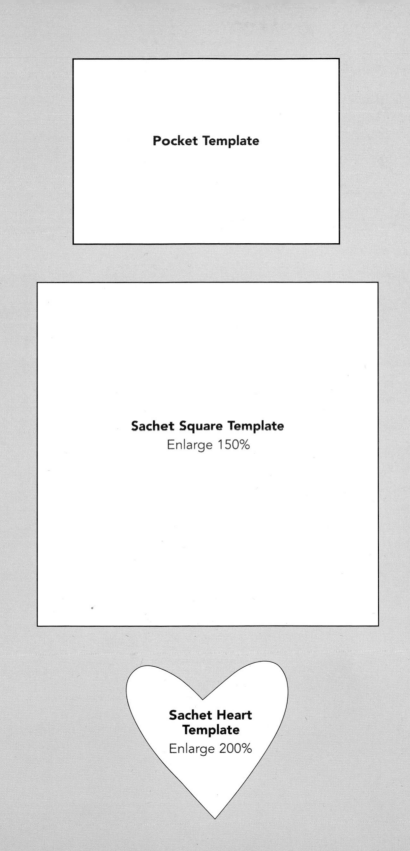

Pocket Template

Sachet Square Template
Enlarge 150%

**Sachet Heart
Template**
Enlarge 200%

Contributors

Karina Hittle

Pages 42, 46, 50, 54, 56, 60, 76, 80, 86, 94, 98, 102, 104, 108, 110, 112

Karina Hittle is an award-winning quilt artist and pattern designer who enjoys all types of needle arts, including sewing, quilting, punch needle, cross stitching, knitting, and crocheting.

After more than 25 years of experience in needle arts, Karina has combined all of her artistic interests into the founding of Artful Offerings™ www.artfulofferings.com, an online resource for quilt and felt patterns as well as a gallery of Karina's artwork.

Karina lives in northern Massachusetts with her husband and business manager, Audie.

Cynthia Shaffer

Pages 32, 34, 38, 72

Mixed-media artist Cynthia Shaffer has been published in *Altered Couture, Material Visions, Somerset Studio, Stamper Sampler, Take Ten,* and *Transparent Art.* Cynthia lives in a beautiful old farmhouse in Orange, California, with her husband, Scott, two sons, Corry and Cameron, and her dearly beloved pup, Stella.

METRIC EQUIVALENCY CHARTS

inches to millimeters and centimeters
(mm-millimeters, cm-centimeters)

inches	mm	cm	inches	cm	inches	cm
⅛	3	0.3	9	22.9	30	76.2
¼	6	0.6	10	25.4	31	78.7
½	13	1.3	12	30.5	33	83.8
⅝	16	1.6	13	33.0	34	86.4
¾	19	1.9	14	35.6	35	88.9
⅞	22	2.2	15	38.1	36	91.4
1	25	2.5	16	40.6	37	94.0
1¼	32	3.2	17	43.2	38	96.5
1½	38	3.8	18	45.7	39	99.1
1¾	44	4.4	19	48.3	40	101.6
2	51	5.1	20	50.8	41	104.1
2½	64	6.4	21	53.3	42	106.7
3	76	7.6	22	55.9	43	109.2
3½	89	8.9	23	58.4	44	111.8
4	102	10.2	24	61.0	45	114.3
4½	114	11.4	25	63.5	46	116.8
5	127	12.7	26	66.0	47	119.4
6	152	15.2	27	68.6	48	121.9
7	178	17.8	28	71.1	49	124.5
8	203	20.3	29	73.7	50	127.0

yards to meters

yards	meters	yards	meters	yards	meters	yards	meters	yards	meters
⅛	0.11	2⅛	1.94	4⅛	3.77	6⅛	5.60	8⅛	7.43
¼	0.23	2¼	2.06	4¼	3.89	6¼	5.72	8¼	7.54
⅜	0.34	2⅜	2.17	4⅜	4.00	6⅜	5.83	8⅜	7.66
½	0.46	2½	2.29	4½	4.11	6½	5.94	8½	7.77
⅝	0.57	2⅝	2.40	4⅝	4.23	6⅝	6.06	8⅝	7.89
¾	0.69	2¾	2.51	4¾	4.34	6¾	6.17	8¾	8.00
⅞	0.80	2⅞	2.63	4⅞	4.46	6⅞	6.29	8⅞	8.12
1	0.91	3	2.74	5	4.57	7	6.40	9	8.23
1⅛	1.03	3⅛	2.86	5⅛	4.69	7⅛	6.52	9⅛	8.34
1¼	1.14	3¼	2.97	5¼	4.80	7¼	6.63	9¼	8.46
1⅜	1.26	3⅜	3.09	5⅜	4.91	7⅜	6.74	9⅜	8.57
1½	1.37	3½	3.20	5½	5.03	7½	6.86	9½	8.69
1⅝	1.49	3⅝	3.31	5⅝	5.14	7⅝	6.97	9⅝	8.80
1¾	1.60	3¾	3.43	5¾	5.26	7¾	7.09	9¾	8.92
1⅞	1.71	3⅞	3.54	5⅞	5.37	7⅞	7.20	9⅞	9.03
2	1.83	4	3.66	6	5.49	8	7.32	10	9.14

INDEX